String Art
Program to draw Spiral Square Pattern

By

Jino Antony

Acknowledgement

There are a lot of people to Thank who made this happen. It was very difficult to accomplish this task and all of them helped and supported me to make this happen. Very much thanks to everyone for your help and support.

Contents

Introduction

String art is basically "connecting two points with a string", as simple as that. String art is one of the most satisfying art in the world. The main attractiveness of this art is, you don't need high level training or knowledge to start doing it which makes it very easy. The result of this is very satisfying even if it is a simple task to complete a string art design. Anyone at any age can start doing string art.

The String Art patterns like String Art geometric patterns can be in any shape. Some examples are: String Art Circle Pattern, String Art triangle pattern, String Art Rectangle Pattern, String Art Square Pattern, String Art Star Pattern, String Art Pentagon pattern, String Art Hexagon Pattern, String Art Octagon Pattern.

The String Art designs can be used for various decorations, some of them are mentioned here:
String Art designs for Table decorations, String Art designs for Room decorations, String Art designs for Wall decorations, String Art designs for Stage decorations, String Art designs for Marriage decorations, String Art designs for Auditorium decorations

The String Art ideas can be implemented anywhere. Some of them are mentioned below: String Art on Canvas, String Art designs on paper, String Art designs on wood, String Art on cardboard, String Art on wall, and String art on thermocol.

I have started and completed some string art designs and it helped me to relax and entertain myself. After creating some designs it became my hobby. It is one of the very satisfying art which anyone can start. I decided to make this book to share my experience and knowledge with everyone who is reading this book. I'm sure that some of you will get the same experience when doing string art.

Contact

If anyone wants to have more designs and do this string art or if you need custom programming code (C#) for a specific string art design, then please contact.

Please sent an email with the image of the string art design for getting the custom programming code (C#) for the same.

You can also send your thoughts and comments regarding this book which will help me to improve.

Please see the contact details below:

Email Id: ar4j1990@gmail.com

Programming tools used

There are a lot of programming tools we can use to draw string art. I'm using visual studio with c# language.

Software: **Microsoft Visual studio 2010**
Language: **C#**

Spiral Square Pattern

We are going to draw the spiral square pattern design as show in the below figure by using c# program:

Please follow the steps mentioned below to get a good result:

1. Open Visual studio.
2. Create **New project** – select **Windows Forms Applications**

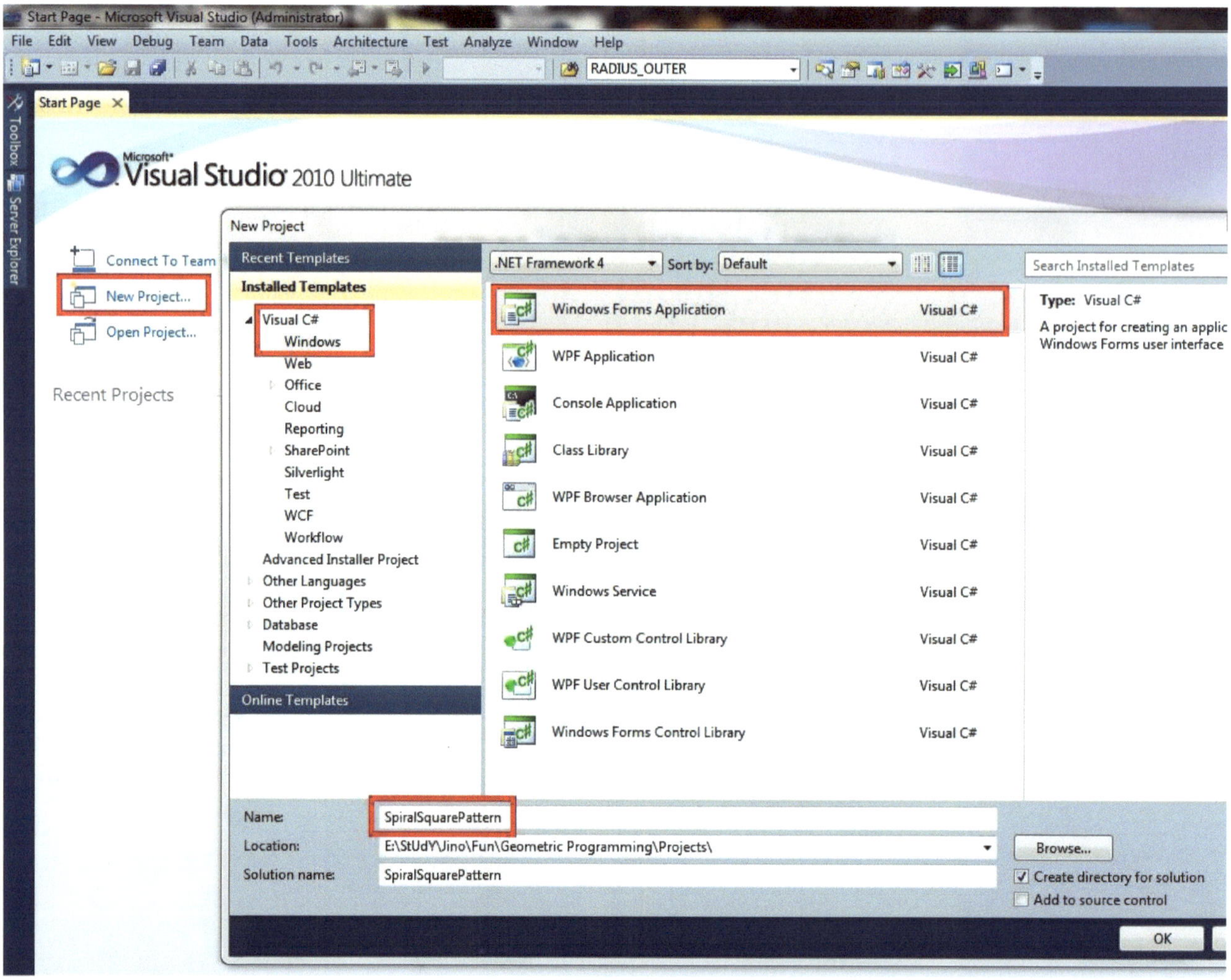

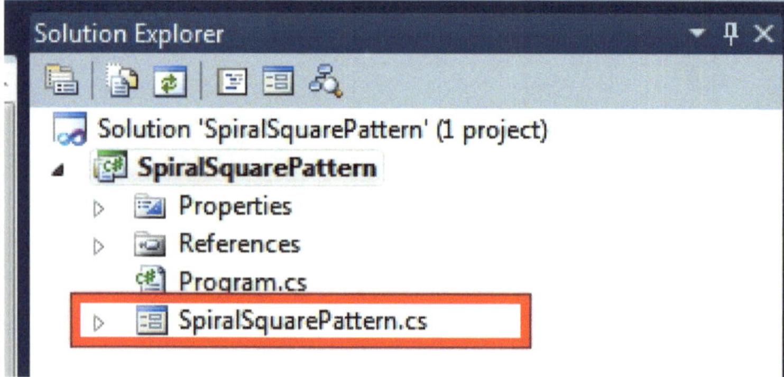

3. I have changes below properties for the default windows form **Form1**
    a. Name changed to **SpiralSquarePattern** from **Form1**

b. Properties:
    i. Text: **Spiral Square Pattern**
    ii. Size: **1920, 1080**

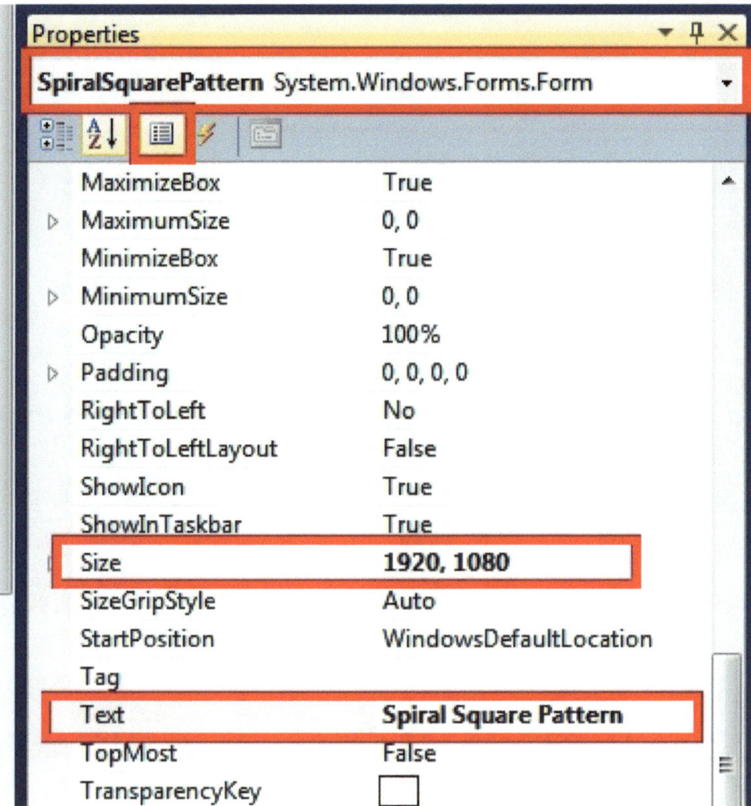

iii. BackColor: **White**

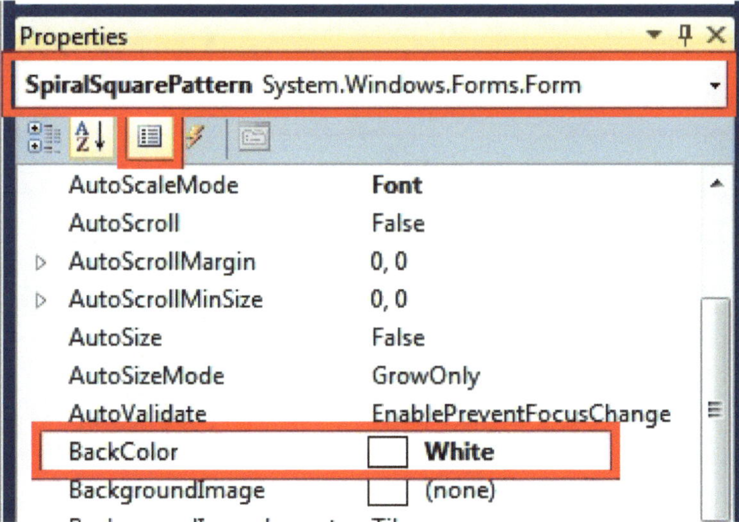

4. Double Click in the Paint event to write the code

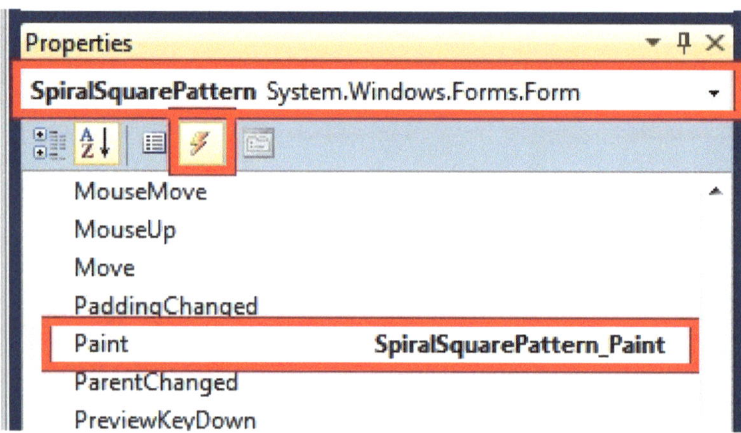

5. Copy and replace the entire code with the below code: (**Highly recommend to type the code line by line by yourself to lean and understand each line**)

```csharp
using System;
using System.Collections.Generic;
using System.ComponentModel;
using System.Data;
using System.Drawing;
using System.Linq;
using System.Text;
using System.Windows.Forms;
using System.Drawing.Drawing2D;

namespace SpiralSquarePattern
{
    public partial class SpiralSquarePattern : Form
    {
        public SpiralSquarePattern()
        {
            InitializeComponent();
        }

        private void SpiralSquarePattern_Paint(object sender, PaintEventArgs e)
        {
            Graphics graphics = e.Graphics;

            graphics.PixelOffsetMode = PixelOffsetMode.HighQuality;
            graphics.SmoothingMode = SmoothingMode.AntiAlias;

            int SquareWidth = 400, lineThickness = 2, distanceBetweenPoints = 10,
countofSquare = 41, delayTimetoDrawLine = 0;
            Color color1, color2, color3, color4;
            Pen pen = new Pen(Color.Black, lineThickness);

            Point SquareStartPoint;

            //Drawing design Layout
```

```csharp
            drawLine(new Point(50, 50), new Point(50, 850), graphics, pen,
delayTimetoDrawLine);
            drawLine(new Point(50, 850), new Point(850, 850), graphics, pen,
delayTimetoDrawLine);
            drawLine(new Point(850, 850), new Point(850, 50), graphics, pen,
delayTimetoDrawLine);
            drawLine(new Point(850, 50), new Point(50, 50), graphics, pen,
delayTimetoDrawLine);
            drawLine(new Point(50, 450), new Point(850, 450), graphics, pen,
delayTimetoDrawLine);
            drawLine(new Point(450, 50), new Point(450, 850), graphics, pen,
delayTimetoDrawLine);

            //Fill Square-1
            SquareStartPoint = new Point(50, 50);
            color1 = Color.LightGray;
            color2 = Color.Blue;
            color3 = Color.Blue;
            color4 = Color.LightGray;
            drawRectangle(SquareStartPoint, SquareWidth, lineThickness,
distanceBetweenPoints, graphics, countofSquare, color1, color2, color3, color4,
delayTimetoDrawLine, pen);

            //Fill Square-2
            SquareStartPoint = new Point(450, 50);
            color1 = Color.Blue;
            color2 = Color.Blue;
            color3 = Color.LightGray;
            color4 = Color.LightGray;
            drawRectangle(SquareStartPoint, SquareWidth, lineThickness,
distanceBetweenPoints, graphics, countofSquare, color1, color2, color3, color4,
delayTimetoDrawLine, pen);

            //Fill Square-3
            SquareStartPoint = new Point(50, 450);
            color1 = Color.LightGray;
            color2 = Color.LightGray;
            color3 = Color.Blue;
            color4 = Color.Blue;
            drawRectangle(SquareStartPoint, SquareWidth, lineThickness,
distanceBetweenPoints, graphics, countofSquare, color1, color2, color3, color4,
delayTimetoDrawLine, pen);

            //Fill Square-4
            SquareStartPoint = new Point(450, 450);
            color1 = Color.Blue;
            color2 = Color.LightGray;
            color3 = Color.LightGray;
            color4 = Color.Blue;
            drawRectangle(SquareStartPoint, SquareWidth, lineThickness,
distanceBetweenPoints, graphics, countofSquare, color1, color2, color3, color4,
delayTimetoDrawLine, pen);
        }

        public void drawRectangle(Point SquareStartPoint, int width, int lineThickness,
int distanceBetweenPoints, Graphics graphics, int countofSquare, Color color1, Color
color2, Color color3, Color color4, int delayTimetoDrawLine, Pen pen)
        {
```

```csharp
            Point nextPoint, temp;
            Point SquarePointA = new Point(SquareStartPoint.X, SquareStartPoint.Y);
            Point SquarePointB = new Point(SquareStartPoint.X, SquareStartPoint.Y +
width);
            Point SquarePointC = new Point(SquareStartPoint.X + width, SquareStartPoint.Y
+ width);
            Point SquarePointD = new Point(SquareStartPoint.X + width,
SquareStartPoint.Y);

            //Outer Square
            {
                pen = new Pen(color1, lineThickness);
                drawLine(new Point(SquareStartPoint.X, SquareStartPoint.Y), new
Point(SquareStartPoint.X, SquareStartPoint.Y + width), graphics, pen,
delayTimetoDrawLine);
                pen = new Pen(color2, lineThickness);
                drawLine(new Point(SquareStartPoint.X, SquareStartPoint.Y + width), new
Point(SquareStartPoint.X + width, SquareStartPoint.Y + width), graphics, pen,
delayTimetoDrawLine);
                pen = new Pen(color3, lineThickness);
                drawLine(new Point(SquareStartPoint.X + width, SquareStartPoint.Y +
width), new Point(SquareStartPoint.X + width, SquareStartPoint.Y), graphics, pen,
delayTimetoDrawLine);
                pen = new Pen(color4, lineThickness);
                drawLine(new Point(SquareStartPoint.X + width, SquareStartPoint.Y), new
Point(SquareStartPoint.X, SquareStartPoint.Y), graphics, pen, delayTimetoDrawLine);
            }

            //Drawing Inner Squares...
            for (int i = 0; i < countofSquare; i++)
            {
                findLineCordinates(SquarePointA, SquarePointB, distanceBetweenPoints, out
nextPoint);
                temp = SquarePointA;
                SquarePointA = nextPoint;
                findLineCordinates(SquarePointB, SquarePointC, distanceBetweenPoints, out
nextPoint);
                SquarePointB = nextPoint;
                findLineCordinates(SquarePointC, SquarePointD, distanceBetweenPoints, out
nextPoint);
                SquarePointC = nextPoint;
                findLineCordinates(SquarePointD, temp, distanceBetweenPoints, out
nextPoint);
                SquarePointD = nextPoint;

                //Inner Square
                pen = new Pen(color1, lineThickness);
                drawLine(SquarePointA, SquarePointB, graphics, pen, delayTimetoDrawLine);
                pen = new Pen(color2, lineThickness);
                drawLine(SquarePointB, SquarePointC, graphics, pen, delayTimetoDrawLine);
                pen = new Pen(color3, lineThickness);
                drawLine(SquarePointC, SquarePointD, graphics, pen, delayTimetoDrawLine);
                pen = new Pen(color4, lineThickness);
                drawLine(SquarePointD, SquarePointA, graphics, pen, delayTimetoDrawLine);
            }
        }
```

```csharp
        //To find the co-ordinates in a line from starting point: distance is given from starting point
        public void findLineCordinates(Point a, Point b, int distanceBetweenPoints, out Point nextPoint)
        {
            double lineLength = 0, distanceRatio = 0;

            lineLength = Math.Sqrt(((b.X - a.X) * (b.X - a.X)) + ((b.Y - a.Y) * (b.Y - a.Y)));
            distanceRatio = distanceBetweenPoints / lineLength;

            nextPoint = new Point((int)(((1 - distanceRatio) * a.X) + (distanceRatio * b.X)), (int)(((1 - distanceRatio) * a.Y) + (distanceRatio * b.Y)));
        }

        //To Draw a line for the given points
        public void drawLine(Point a, Point b, Graphics graphics, Pen pen, int delayTimetoDrawLine)
        {
            System.Threading.Thread.Sleep(delayTimetoDrawLine);
            graphics.DrawLine(pen, a, b);
        }
    }
}
```

Spiral Square

We are going to draw the spiral square design as show in the below figure by using c# program:

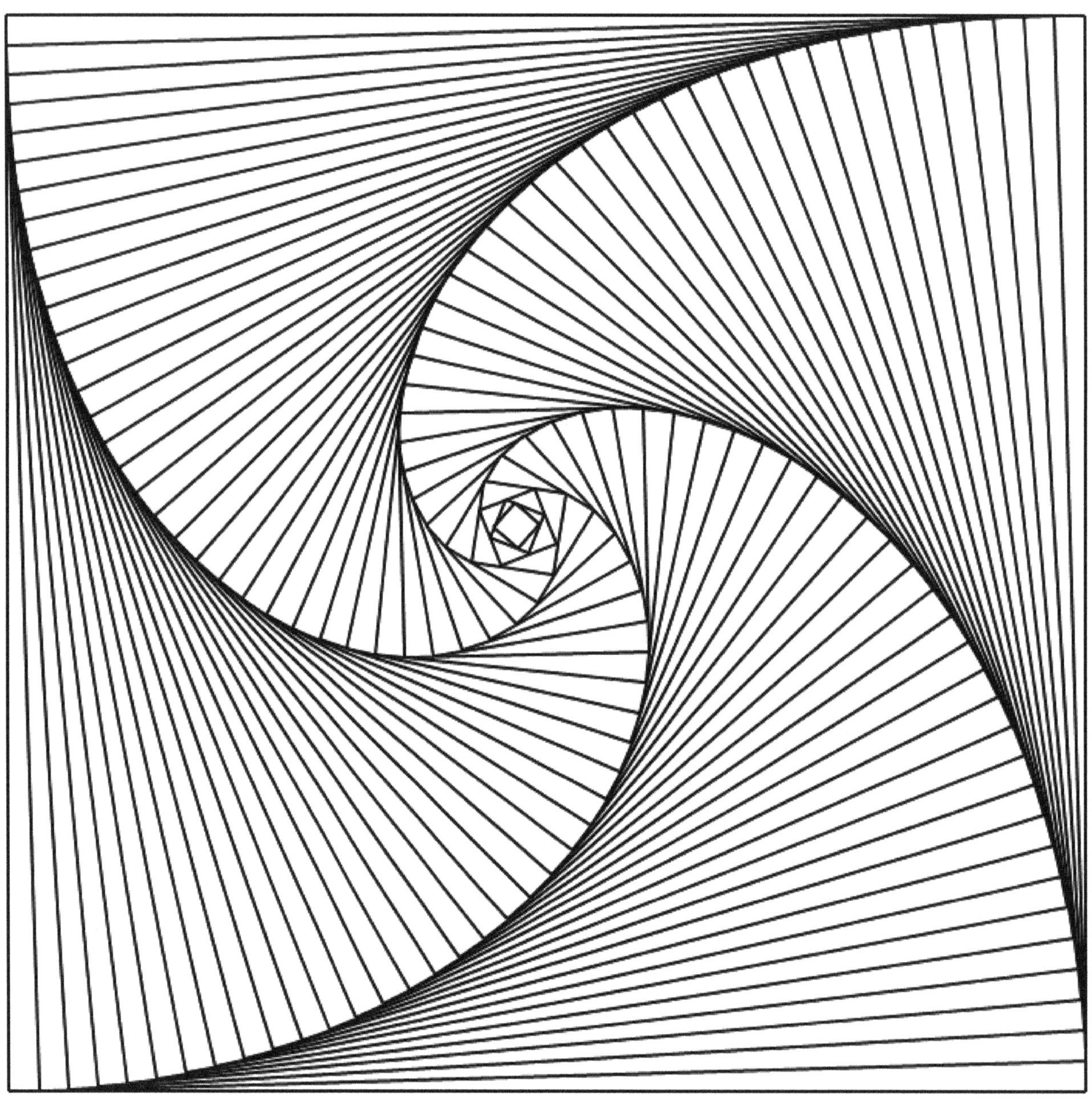

Please follow the steps mentioned below to get a good result:

1. Open Visual studio.
2. Create **New project** – select **Windows Forms Applications**

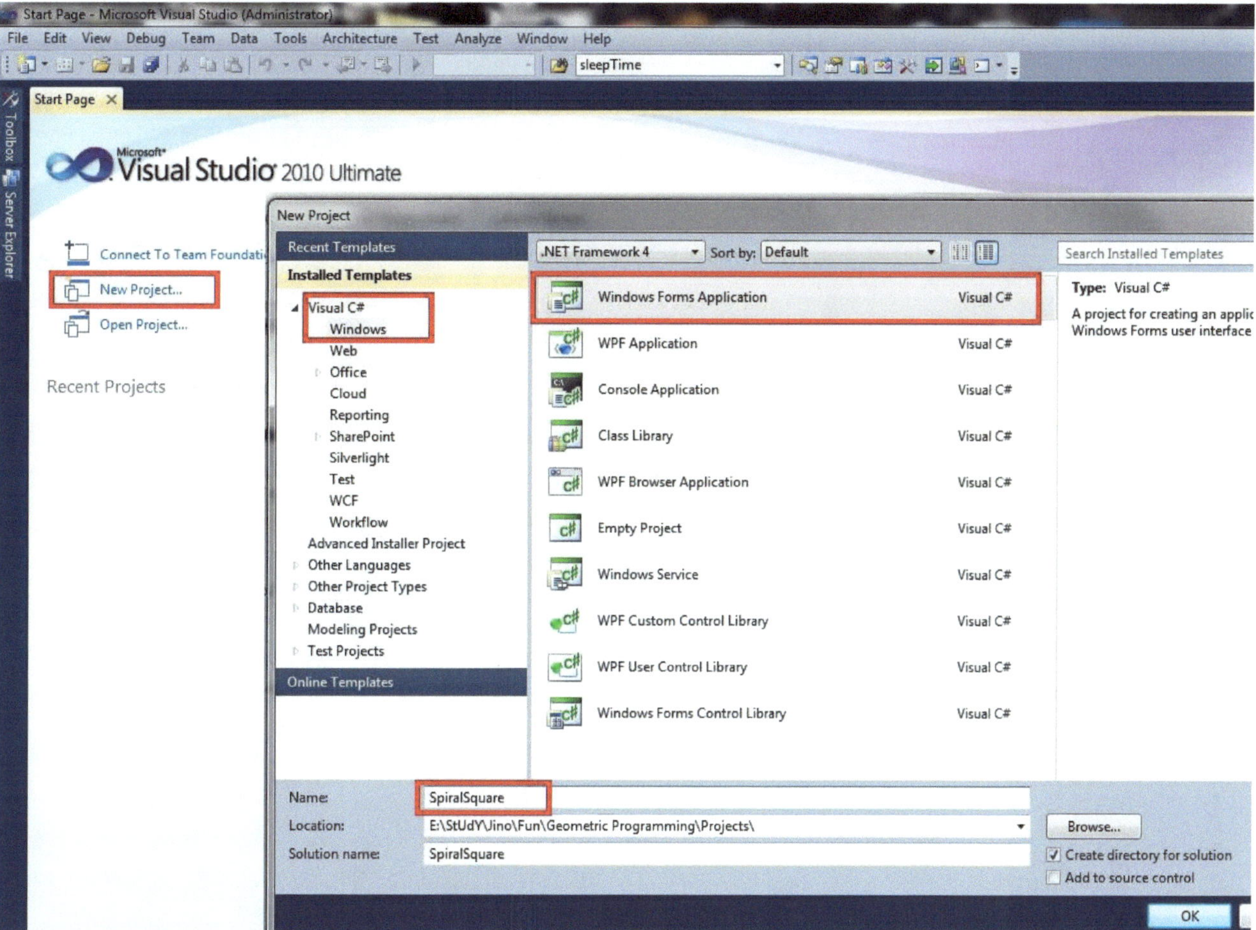

3. I have changes below properties for the default windows form **Form1**
   a. Name changed to **SpiralSquare** from **Form1**

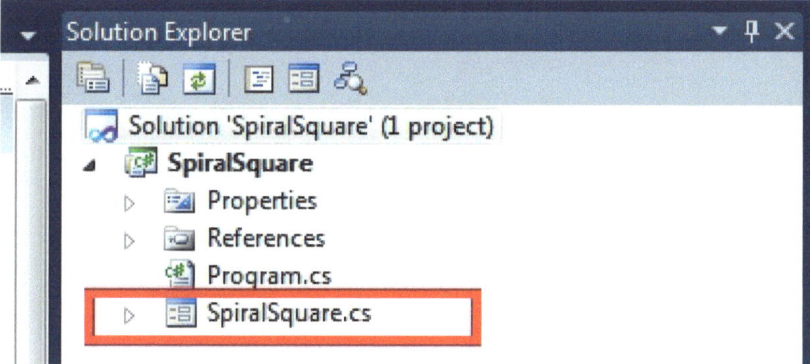

    b. Properties:
       i. Text: **Spiral Square**
      ii. Size: **1920, 1080**

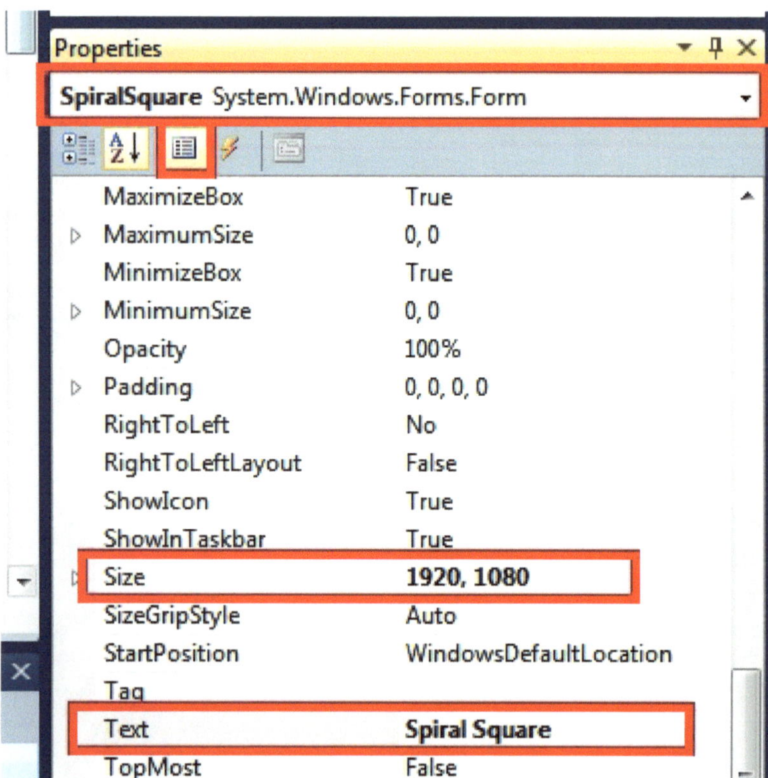

      iii. BackColor: **White**

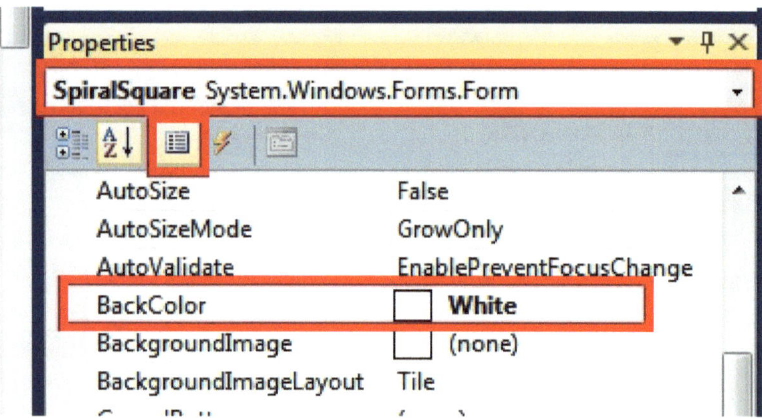

4. Double Click in the Paint event to write the code

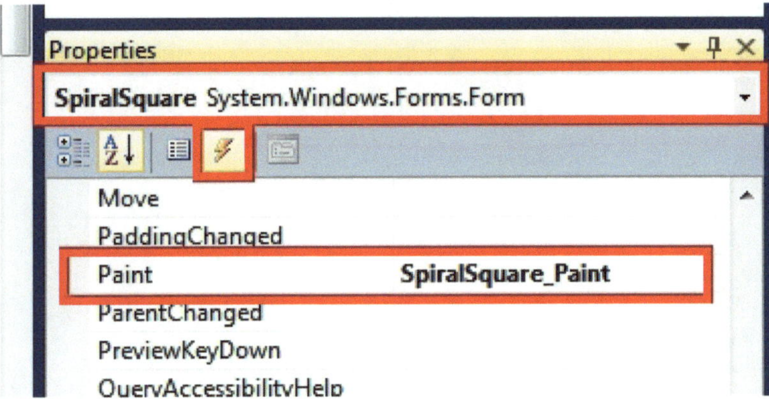

5. Copy and replace the entire code with the below code: (**Highly recommend to type the code line by line by yourself to lean and understand each line**)

```csharp
using System;
using System.Collections.Generic;
using System.ComponentModel;
using System.Data;
using System.Drawing;
using System.Linq;
using System.Text;
using System.Windows.Forms;
using System.Drawing.Drawing2D; //For Drawing smooth lines

namespace SpiralSquare
{
    public partial class SpiralSquare : Form
    {
        public SpiralSquare()
        {
            InitializeComponent();
        }

        private void SpiralSquare_Paint(object sender, PaintEventArgs e)
        {
            //==========================DRAW SPIRAL SQUARE==========================

            Graphics graphics = e.Graphics;

            graphics.PixelOffsetMode = PixelOffsetMode.HighQuality;
            graphics.SmoothingMode = SmoothingMode.AntiAlias;

            int RectangleWidth = 700, lineThickness = 2, distanceBetweenPoints = 20,
countOfInnerSquares = 37, DelayTimetoDrawLines = 10;

            Color color = Color.Black;
            Pen pen = new Pen(color, lineThickness);

            Point a = new Point(50, 50);
```

```csharp
            Point topLeftPoint = new Point(a.X, a.Y);
            Point bottomLeftPoint = new Point(a.X, a.Y + RectangleWidth);
            Point bottomRightPoint = new Point(a.X + RectangleWidth, a.Y +
RectangleWidth);
            Point topRightPoint = new Point(a.X + RectangleWidth, a.Y);

            Point nextPoint, temp;

            //System.Threading.Thread.Sleep(DelayTimetoDrawLines);

            //Outer Rectangle
            drawLine(new Point(a.X, a.Y), new Point(a.X, a.Y + RectangleWidth), graphics,
pen, DelayTimetoDrawLines);
            drawLine(new Point(a.X, a.Y + RectangleWidth), new Point(a.X +
RectangleWidth, a.Y + RectangleWidth), graphics, pen, DelayTimetoDrawLines);
            drawLine(new Point(a.X + RectangleWidth, a.Y + RectangleWidth), new Point(a.X
+ RectangleWidth, a.Y), graphics, pen, DelayTimetoDrawLines);
            drawLine(new Point(a.X + RectangleWidth, a.Y), new Point(a.X, a.Y), graphics,
pen, DelayTimetoDrawLines);

            //Brush b = new SolidBrush(Color.Yellow);
            //graphics.FillRectangle(b, a.X + 1, a.Y + 1, RectangleWidth - 2,
RectangleWidth - 2);

            System.Threading.Thread.Sleep(DelayTimetoDrawLines * 2);

            //Drawing Inner Rectangles...
            for (int i = 0; i < countOfInnerSquares; i++)
            {
                findLineCordinates(topLeftPoint, bottomLeftPoint, distanceBetweenPoints,
out nextPoint);
                temp = topLeftPoint;
                topLeftPoint = nextPoint;
                findLineCordinates(bottomLeftPoint, bottomRightPoint,
distanceBetweenPoints, out nextPoint);
                bottomLeftPoint = nextPoint;
                findLineCordinates(bottomRightPoint, topRightPoint,
distanceBetweenPoints, out nextPoint);
                bottomRightPoint = nextPoint;
                findLineCordinates(topRightPoint, temp, distanceBetweenPoints, out
nextPoint);
                topRightPoint = nextPoint;

                //Inner Rectangle
                drawLine(topLeftPoint, bottomLeftPoint, graphics, pen,
DelayTimetoDrawLines);
                drawLine(bottomLeftPoint, bottomRightPoint, graphics, pen,
DelayTimetoDrawLines);
                drawLine(bottomRightPoint, topRightPoint, graphics, pen,
DelayTimetoDrawLines);
                drawLine(topRightPoint, topLeftPoint, graphics, pen,
DelayTimetoDrawLines);
            }
        }

        //To find the co-ordinates in a line from starting point: distance is given from
starting point
        public void findLineCordinates(Point a, Point b, int distance, out Point t)
```

```csharp
        {
            double lineLength = 0, distanceRatio = 0;

            lineLength = Math.Sqrt(((b.X - a.X) * (b.X - a.X)) + ((b.Y - a.Y) * (b.Y -
a.Y)));
            distanceRatio = distance / lineLength;

            t = new Point((int)(((1 - distanceRatio) * a.X) + (distanceRatio * b.X)),
(int)(((1 - distanceRatio) * a.Y) + (distanceRatio * b.Y)));
        }

    //To Draw a line for the given points
    public void drawLine(Point a, Point b, Graphics graphics, Pen pen, int
DelayTimetoDrawLines)
        {
            System.Threading.Thread.Sleep(DelayTimetoDrawLines);
            graphics.DrawLine(pen, a, b);
        }
    }
}
```

Upcoming String art design projects

I have created some additional string art design for you. I'm sure you can try to draw these designs with the knowledge from this book.

If you wish to get the step by step process for the following designs, let me know by adding the comments when you rate this book.

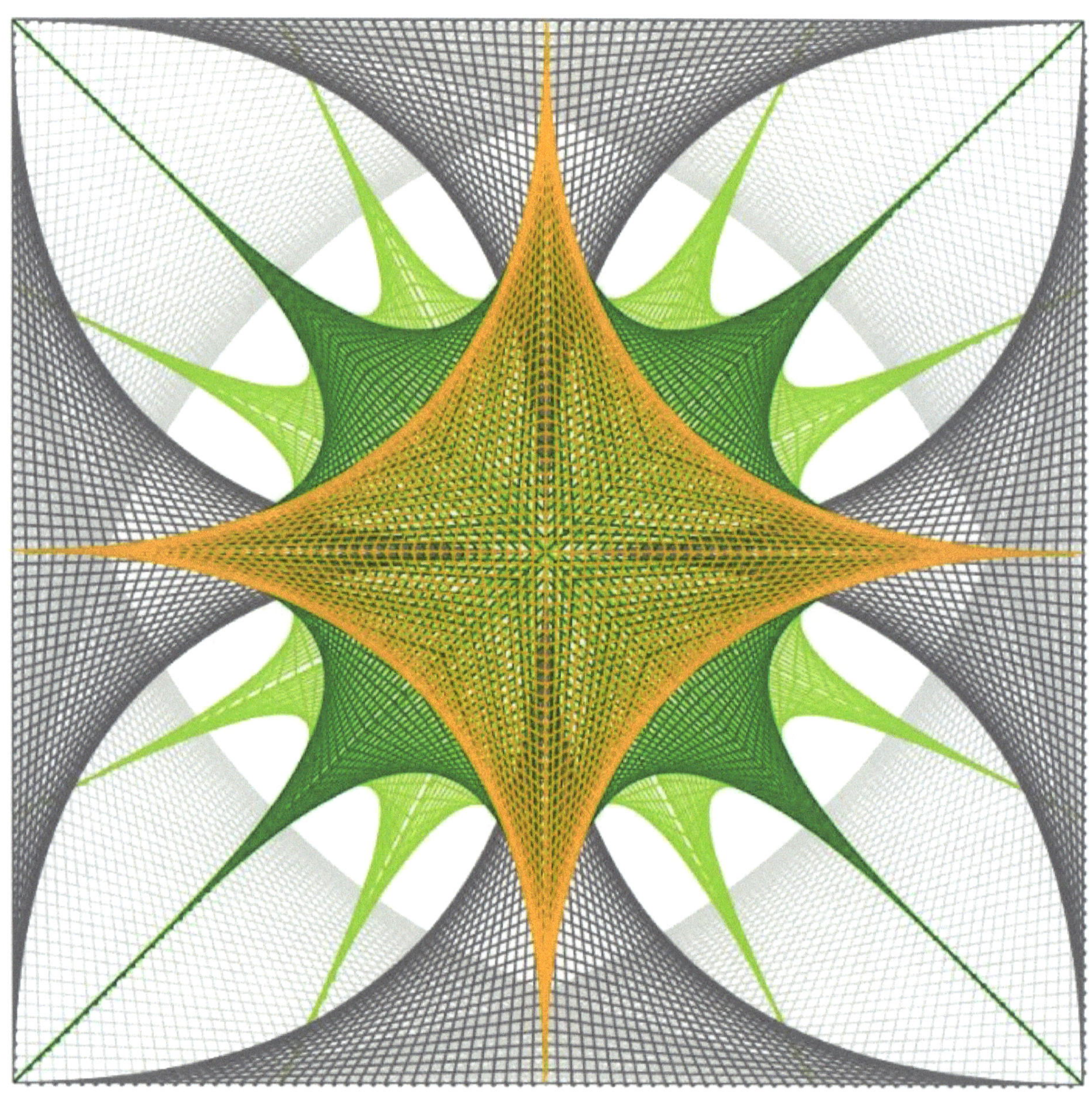

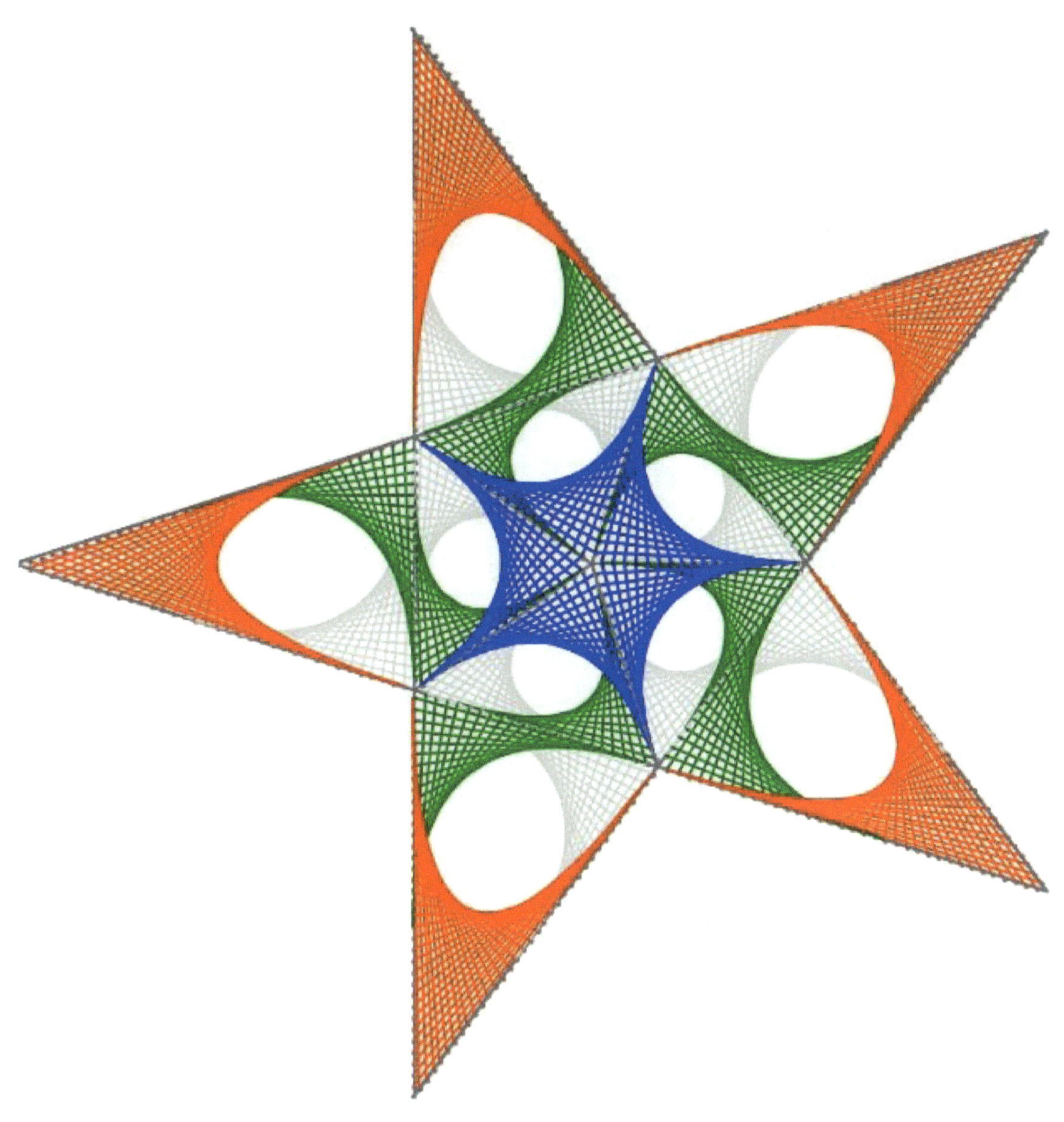

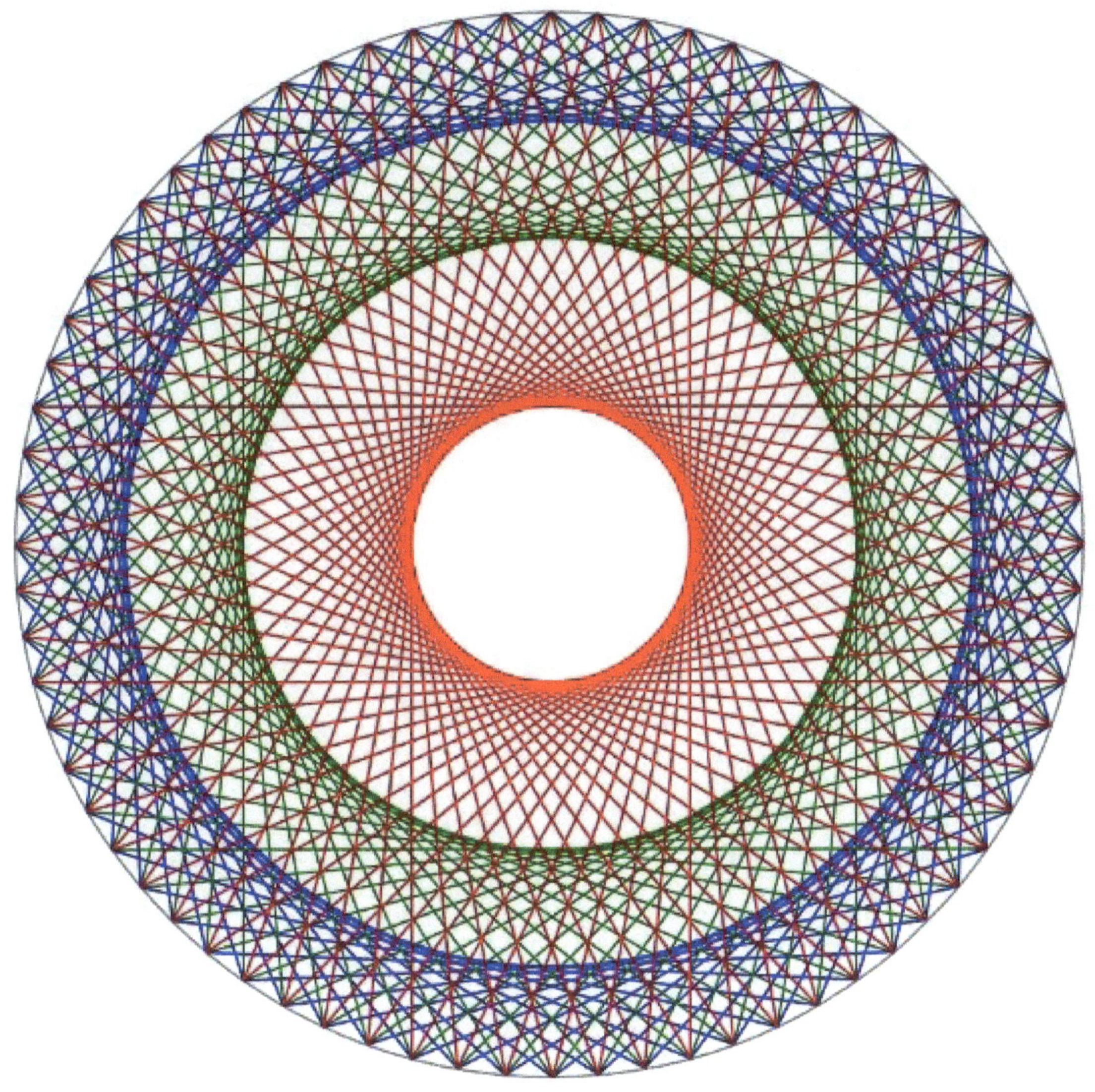

Completed String art design projects

You can buy books or read books in Amazon Kindle for the below string art designs.

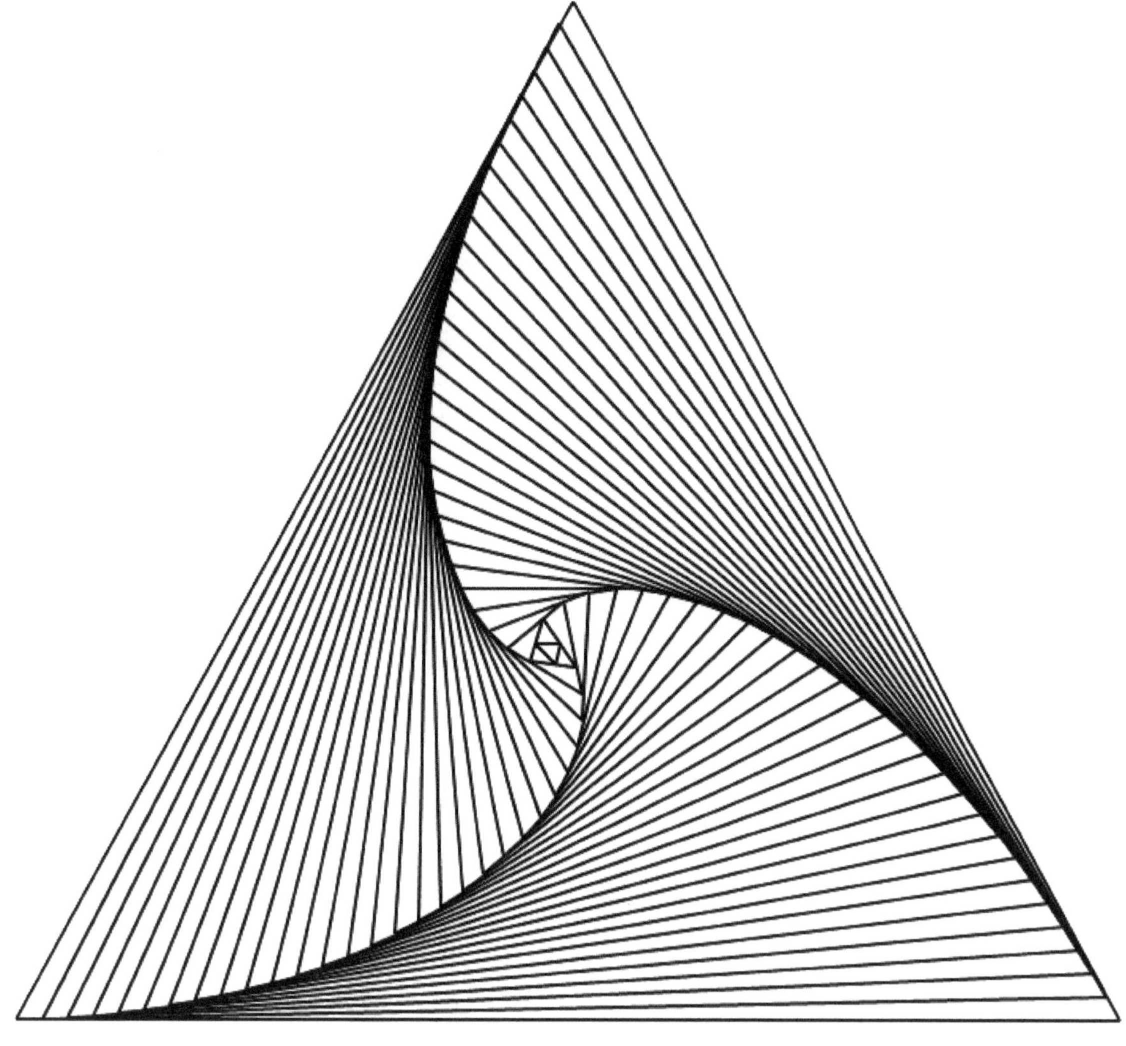

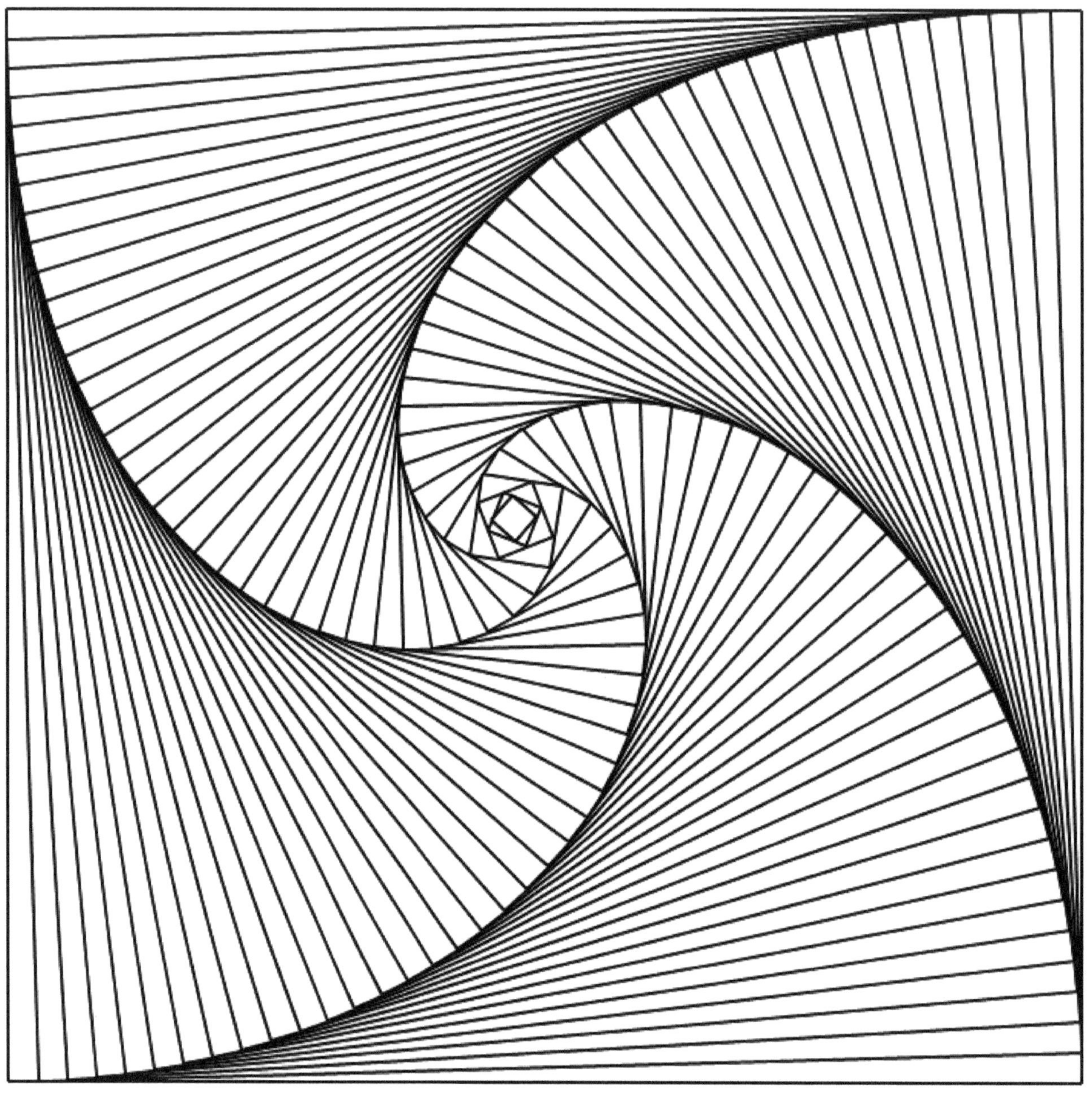